Avoidant Personality Disorder: The Ultimate Guide to Symptoms, Treatment, and Prevention

By: Clayton Geoffreys

Copyright © 2015 by Clayton Geoffreys

All rights reserved. Neither this book nor any portion thereof may be reproduced or used in any manner whatsoever without the express written permission. Published in the United States of America.

Visit my website at www.claytongeoffreys.com
Cover photo by Antranias is licensed under CC BY 3.0 / modified from original

Table of Contents

Foreword 1

Chapter 1: What is Avoidant Personality Disorder? 3

Chapter 2: The Four Subtypes of AvPD 9

    1. Phobic 9

    2. Conflicted 10

    3. Hypersensitivity 11

    4. Self-Deserting 11

Chapter 3: What Causes Avoidant Personality Disorder? 13

Chapter 4: The 9 Most Common Symptoms of AvPD 21

    1. Extreme Sensitivity to Criticism and Remarks 21

    2. Self-Isolation 21

    3. Avoidance of Personal Risks 22

    4. Low Self-Esteem and Views Self as Socially Inept 23

    5. Inhibited in Interpersonal Situations 24

    6. Constantly Focuses on Criticism and Rejection 26

    7. Limited Intimate Relationships 27

    8.   Living through Fantasy 28

    9.   Avoidance of Occupational Interpersonal Situations 30

Chapter 5: Seven Common Therapy Methods for AvPD 32

    1.   Online Support Groups 32

    2.   Group Therapy 33

    3.   Exposure Therapy 33

    4.   Intervention 34

    5.   Cognitive Skills Therapy 36

    6.   Psychological Therapy 37

    7.   Drug Therapy 38

Chapter 6: How to Choose the Right Therapy Approach 41

Chapter 7: How to Overcome AvpD: 7 Steps 48

    1.   Intervention 48

    2.   Admission 49

    3.   Understanding 50

    4.   Symptom Evaluation 52

    5.   Therapy 53

6.	Support	55
7.	Adherence	56

Chapter 8: How to Find Your Escape 59

Conclusion 63

Final Word/About the Author 69

Endnotes 72

Disclaimer

This book is not intended as a substitute for the medical advice of a physician or medical professional. The reader should regularly visit a doctor in matters relating to his or her health and particularly with respect to symptoms that may require medical diagnosis or attention.

Foreword

Personality disorders can significantly alter the way one lives their life. Understanding the symptoms of these disorders is important for everyone. Whether or not you personally suffer from these disorders, learning to recognize symptoms is the first step to being able to best assist someone who may be suffering from a condition. Psychologists have studied disorders for many years, creating multiple iterations of diagnosis tools; it's difficult to truly pinpoint everything with 100% accuracy, but with time and further research, we as a society will become better aware of the nature of these disorders. Hopefully from reading *Avoidant Personality Disorder: The Ultimate Guide to Symptoms, Treatment, and Prevention,* I can pass along some of the abundance of information I have learned about Avoidant Personality Disorder, including its symptoms, therapies to consider, and ways to begin overcoming AvPD. Thank you for downloading my book. Hope you enjoy and if you do, please do not forget to leave a review! Also, check out my website at claytongeoffreys.com to join my exclusive list where I let you know about my latest books. To thank you for your purchase, you can go to my site to download a free copy of *33 Life Lessons: Success Principles, Career Advice & Habits of Successful People*. In the book, you'll learn from some of the greatest thought leaders of different industries on what it takes to become successful and how to live a great life.

Cheers,

Clayton Geoffreys

Chapter 1: What is Avoidant Personality Disorder?

For some people, the simple act of greeting another person can be traumatizing. Facing another person and risking being judged, criticized or rejected is too much. Though this may be on the more extreme end of the problem, Avoidant Personality Disorder (or AvPD) makes situations exactly like this one a reality. AvPD patients are so focused on what other people think of them, that most decide to no longer interact with other people. This in turn can lead to a very lonely and depressing lifestyle, as well as a dangerous one. With the exponential growth of virtual communication, socialization, and interaction, there is both a higher probability as well as an easier way to hide a condition like AvPD. Utilizing the networks, gaming and social, that are available, it is quite easy and common for people to establish a persona very unlike who they are in reality. What results is a group of people with deeply established fears of other people and the acceptance of who they really are in person. This virtual interaction can both enable and hide mental disorders that can grow to be quite severe. Someone with AvPD could use online avatars, profiles, and game characters to create what they believe people would see as an acceptable personality. Though they would know that the created persona is not their actual personality, they would find it easier to interact through them. This would then allow a bigger buildup of dislike and humiliation of themselves as they would see each improvement of the false self as a reflection of the negative aspects of their true self. As confusing as it may seem, this is sometimes the only way people with Avoidant Personality Disorder can relate and interact with others without feeling the exaggerated pressures they find in face to face interactions.

Avoidant Personality Disorder has been broken into four subtypes. There are phobic, conflicted, hypersensitivity, and self-deserting. Each subtype represents a more defined version of the illness and how it affects the patient. Phobic subtypes have an exact fear of something or someone in particular. Conflicted persons tend to find themselves consistently confused by the actions they are to take and the worry that stems from the fear of those actions. Hypersensitives are generally oversensitive to the reactions and information they get from other people or circumstances. Self-deserting is represented by the intentional withdraw of one into themselves and to utilize a fantasy self as reality, even though this increases their perception of their own shortcomings in reality.[1]

There are two possible speculations that cause AvPD. One is genetic and the other is environmental. Genetics focus more on other symptoms that can actually result as a cause of AvPD, like anxiety or depression. Environment can cover anything from traumatic experiences to a neglected childhood. No one cause or definitive reasoning has yet to be fully established. Other conditions that can be attributed to AvPD are schizophrenia, severe depression, suicidal tendencies, bipolar disorder, multiple personality disorder, social anxiety disorder, a plethora of various phobias, and an overall avoidance of contact with people.

Symptoms of Avoidant Personality Disorder come in a wide range simply because it is a multitude of symptoms that have similar components that make up the disorder. The basis of AvPD is the underlying social anxiety disorder. Anxiety can lead to the conflict that in turn leads to the stress and further anxiety. This would result in fear, phobias and depression. When the symptoms combine, it forms a person who is not able to properly function in cohesion with other people. Only in understanding the presence of the individual symptoms can the big picture lead to a diagnosis of Avoidant Personality Disorder.

There are a multitude of different therapies available for people with AvPD. The majority of therapies focuses on helping the person understand their condition and the fact that they are the ones with the capabilities to change how they view things in order to overcome these hindrances. Medication is usually reserved for those who have an underlying depression or anxiety issue. For others, it is more pertinent to help them learn how to socialize with people, how to interact in groups, and how to perceive themselves in a better light.

Avoidant Personality Disorder is a battle within a person to overcome irrational beliefs and fears about themselves and about social interactions. You can still live out your life with AvPD, but will find yourself extremely limited in many aspects. People who cannot find positive inspirations about their own image and how they appear to others will not be able to fully function around others. This can affect everything, from their family and love life to their work environment. Assumptions and fears will cripple them even with the simple idea of socializing. Targeting the initial causes, base issues, and the resulting adherences will allow a therapist or doctor to help the patient move on in life without the looming disorder being so present. Though, like any learned or overly practiced behavior, someone with such an ingrained belief is rarely going to be able to completely overcome how they feel about themselves and other people.

Chapter 2: The Four Subtypes of AvPD

1. Phobic

Phobias are the fear of something or someone. It could be a person, a situation, an object or even an idea; phobias are something a person will struggle to overcome and have as a part of their life. Phobias of people, of how other people respond to someone, of public places, of crowds, etc., are the basis of the phobic subtype of Avoidant Personality Disorder. With this illness, you will actually fear the people or situations that allow for socializing. These fears will lead to an unsubstantiated belief that the person or situation is actually harmful to you in one way or another. This in return will lead to an avoidance of the people or situations. The result is someone who is almost crippled by the fight or flight reaction to, in fact, run from it. Having the body's ingrained response of flight being fulfilled by running away or staying away will then feed into the lack of positive self-image. Low self-esteem will then lead to depression and an even more negative outlook of the person's own self.

2. Conflicted

Confliction subtypes arise when you feel that you are at a constant mental war with yourself over the actions you should make and the assumed outcomes of those reactions. Because a person with AvPD will rarely see a positive outcome in being socially active, they do not see a situation that will not hurt them. The indecisive nature of AvPD is a result of the preconceived notions of rejection and humiliation they think will occur if they make the wrong choice. Thus the wrong choice, in every situation, will be to act at all. Once again, such persons find themselves at a stalemate on what exactly they should do to successfully thwart any harm coming to them, be it mental or physical.

3. Hypersensitivity

People take criticism, comments, and body language in different ways. There is also a varied response in how bad or well someone is able to handle any such remarks or actions. With hypersensitivity, they would tend to over-react or display an extreme reaction to how people respond to them and how they take what that response is. What may seem like a silly offhanded remark may seriously impact someone with hypersensitivity. Feeling deeply wounded over words or gestures can cause a person to feel rejection on a more severe level. This will then cause increased stress, anxiety, and/or depression, giving them more of a reason to avoid contact with other people. Someone suffering from this would often be seen as over-emotional or over-reactors and such labels alone can be detrimental to their emotional well-being.

4. Self-Deserting

Virtual worlds and online social interaction is plentiful

now. For someone with AvPD, this is both a blessing and a curse. Self-deserting subtypes will withdraw from reality and gain a false deniability about themselves in preference to living in a fantasy realm. Often they have alternative personalities or characters that they attempt to live vicariously through, all the while seeing themselves as even less because of how they measure up to the fantasy persona. The idea that their own issues are outside of themselves, or away, when they are these characters, allows them to ignore the underlying issues and to build-up a more negative outlook on whom they really are. By being "someone else," they feel like they can disconnect from the issues they would normally feel in themselves. This can lead to forms of bipolar disorder, schizophrenia, and even multiple personality disorder. Accepting the idea of them being someone else makes it easier to downplay the severity of what is actually occurring in their psyche to make them need this other persona.

Chapter 3: What Causes Avoidant Personality Disorder?

Avoidant Personality Disorder involves a cluster of issues with similar or shared attributes. Primarily, AvPD is a behavioral issue more than a medical one. Though AvPD can lead to medical issues, the root cause is often psychological. There are multiple theories on where, exactly, AvPD stems from. Some aspects of the disorder can evolve from genetic predispositions for anxiety and depression-based issues. Both anxiety and depression can lay a solid foundation for the paranoia and self-depreciation to evolve from. Childhood abuse, neglect, and trauma can also result in conditions that will contribute to or become Avoidant Personality Disorder. Someone that has been raised under constant humiliation, rejection, and neglect will come to expect the reaction to be universal. With such a negative expectation, withdrawal from people and society occurs and eventually enhances the previous fears and beliefs about these interactions. The cycle continues to build upon itself and enhance the severity of the disorder.

Dr. Phillip Long published research stating that there are a multitude of studies of the causes being environmental, genetic, and/or prenatal. A brief explanation of the sociology of primates is given to create a basis for understanding the different creation of these traits. The understanding of how genetic disorders are passed down, how the young is treated, and how the group acts as a whole can reflect on the human reality of how sociological avoidances can grow.[2]

The genetic disposition is only the first factor, as it is not always present nor is it necessary. With genetics, having a trait from both parents is a known logic. If both parents have the trait, the likelihood of the offspring carrying the trait is higher. If both parents have a trait for depressive disorders, there is a high probability that the child will also have depression issues. This is also the same for anxiety-based traits. A blurred area of this is that if the parent has disorders that affect how they perceive people and social interactions, these will be reflected in the way they raise their young. So even if the child has not actually gained a trait for depression or anxiety, the behavior will still be learned from how the parent reacts in regards to these conditions. Depression and anxiety can be psychological or an imbalance in certain chemical processes of the brain. Chemical imbalances are a physiological condition and are much more likely to be passed on to the offspring, whereas the psychological forms of depression and anxiety are more of a learned behavior or one created in response to outside influences. The psychological forms of depression and anxiety are often a learned behavior and are perceived as genetic because of the prevalence of the offspring to have the conditions of the parent.

Again, the condition is just as likely to be something the child becomes accustomed to because of the parent, as such is something that they actually genetically received as a trait.

Early mistreatment or neglect can lead to an expectation of such behavior. Children that are raised in an abusive environment, whether it is physical abuse, sexual abuse, neglect, or the mere observation of any of those factors, will often be strongly affected by such. Abuse and neglect can be dealt with in different ways. Some people will turn to crime and substance abuse, some will repeat the behaviors on their own children, and some will withdraw. Withdrawal can be the starting point of something like AvPD. The child grows up learning that people hurt them, physically or mentally, and that the safest bet is to stay away from them altogether. Childhood events happen when the mind is most pliable and can make overcoming issues resulting from this time much more difficult.

Traumatic events can often lead to serious psychological complications. When a person experiences a moment where they are severely humiliated, rejected, or demeaned in any fashion, the psychological fallout can change the person's view of many aspects of their lives. If the person already suffers from insecurity issues or has hypersensitivity problems, the event can become the pivotal point in which they change how they proceed. Examples of this can be seen with the "15 minutes of fame" crowd. YouTube sensations are a common event and with this come people posting all kinds of videos to the website. When a particularly embarrassing video, such as one in which someone is physically assaulted or inebriated, it is easy for a large expanse of people to view and comment on the video. The person is then subjected to cruelty, humiliation, and hurt from the populace that observes and participates in the furthering of the video. That person would then begin to fear running into people who may have seen the video, on or off line. The avoidance comes and they begin to withdraw from society. Avoidance of public places, then of groups, and then of individuals could occur. As the degradation of the person's perception of people continues, the probability of Avoidant Personality Disorder grows. This example is one of many that can be attributed to the nature of people as a whole presently. Nothing can fully ensure that a person would not be subjected to this kind of reaction anymore. With such easy ways of hurting people indirectly, more people are likely to be cruel and vulgar and thus more people are likely to be hurt by it.

Not to say that an Internet video is the worst or least cause of traumatic events, only that it is becoming one of the most common. Some stream hosts have recently released videos explaining how owning a stream could have detrimental effects on the host themselves. One such host (name is left out for content purposes) narrates and breaks down first person shooter games. He recently released a video in which he talks about why he no longer interacts with his viewers. Many viewers will request certain walkthroughs or specific information about something. Some will beg for monetary assistance or promotion of their own feeds. As a host assists one or two, more expect the same treatment. The more interactive they are with their followers, the more that is asked of them and the harsher the reactions of rejection become. The host will then withdraw from the communication, and in some instances, even withdraw from fellow hosts that they do joint videos with. This is really not even close to the severity of the damage people can do in such situations. There have been instances of this getting much more severe, to the point of stalking and even physical reactions from people. As the situations get increasingly dangerous, or even just psychologically difficult to overcome, the person will find themselves withdrawing from people. For people like stream hosts, this can cause loss of content, followers, and eventually, their job.

Chapter 4: The 9 Most Common Symptoms of AvPD

1. Extreme Sensitivity to Criticism and Remarks

Hypersensitivity is a subtype of AvPD, but it is also a present symptom in all forms of AvPD. Someone who has a condition revolving around the perceptions of themselves, reactions of other people, and phobias will have a certain level of sensitivity to come to these extreme conclusions. Patients with AvPD will see a joke as someone making fun of them and would take it personally. Anything said in response to someone with AvPD will invariably be perceived as much harsher and crueler than it was originally intended to be.

2. Self-Isolation

Isolating one's self from places and other people is a result of AvPD, and as such is an obvious symptom. By completely cutting themselves off from everyone, they feel the safest and less likely to experience the negative aspects of social interaction. This can lead to a dangerous lifestyle, especially if depression is a dominant key in the person's psychological symptoms. They can get to a point of such isolation that no one knows where or how they are doing. Being without any socialization whatsoever can lead to other habits and negative psychological reactions that can impact the person's well-being and personal life.

3. Avoidance of Personal Risks

People take personal risks constantly. One faces a risk even just introducing themselves to someone new with the possibility that the person would not reciprocate pleasantries or would just turn out to be a negative person to meet. A risk such as this is extremely common, and yet, to someone with AvPD, this is a risk not worth taking. With that in mind, personal risks are involved in interviewing for a job, going to the store where there are people shopping, walking in a park surrounded with people, or any other situation in which human interaction can occur. These risks are something necessary to develop personal character, social skill, and to open up new opportunities (such as a job or friendship). Without taking these risks, many opportunities and learning experiences are missed.

4. Low Self-Esteem and Views Self as Socially Inept

People will have a hard time receiving positive input from other people if they cannot find anything positive about themselves. Having low self-esteem can lead to the belief that one is incapable of socially interacting with other people. The cycle of negativity grows off of this perception. If a person sees them as less of anything comparatively, then they will assume and expect negativity in response. With the issues that already press down on someone with AvPD, this own idea of low self-worth is amplified and applied to what they are already perceiving as disdain and disrespect from others. Self-esteem is not necessarily a sense of thinking one is better than anyone else; it is simply the acknowledgement that a person has both good and bad attributes and accepting all of them equally. Low self-esteem would result in one seeing no positive attributes. This creates the idea that they are incapable of social reaction because they are incapable of relating to anyone else's ideas and responses. Again, the symptoms begin to stack up.

5. Inhibited in Interpersonal Situations

Inhibition can be a good thing. Knowing when you should hold back or hesitating to move forward with certain actions or strong opinions is a good self-control mechanism. Inhibiting yourself in any situation with another person, however, can have bad outcomes, ones that are increased by other symptoms of AvPD. Inhibitions can cause a person to seem weak or even sociopathic. Weakness is a conclusion drawn from the inaction of the person to move forward with relationships, activities, and the like, that arise in social situations. Normally, sociopathic natures are not that at all, but only the conclusion drawn by ignorant individuals that cannot understand a person's unwillingness to make certain socially acceptable actions/reactions. For instance, being unwilling to kiss an intimate partner for fear of rejection causes the individual to be inhibited in being intimate. The partner may perceive this inhibition as a refusal or a denial to get that level of attention. The person inhibiting themselves is then accused of not feeling or understanding the feelings of the other person. There is a bit of irony in this symptom as refusing to be active or reactive in certain situations can then cause them to reject or humiliate other people. This is not to say though that inhibitions only affect the other person. Inhibitions, like risks, are situations that open up new possibilities and can strengthen or weaken bonds with other people. Refusing to relinquish these inhibitions, therefore, further inhibits one from trying new things or moving forward with something new in their life.

6. Constantly Focuses on Criticism and Rejection

People often give each other constructive criticism, joke nonchalantly about meaningless issues, or turn down others for various reasons. Avoidant Personality Disorder patients tend to hang on to these and amplify their meanings. Regardless if the person has complimented them, let them down gently, or was intending a more positive reaction, AvPD patients are going to focus on the negative aspect and may even obsess over them. There is even an expectation for interactions to be negative, and so the person will go into a social setting already worried and focusing on every conceived look or statement. Their focus on the idea of criticism and rejection causes them to overlook anything good that can come of the situation. The continued focus and obsession will grow into a bigger issue than it actually is. Pessimism is taken to a much darker area when it is as consistent as it is in someone with AvPD.

7. Limited Intimate Relationships

One of the problems with avoiding people is the limited possibility of forming relationships on a personal and intimate level with other people. In avoiding the chance of this even happening, someone with Avoidant Personality Disorder prevent themselves from building such relationships. Even after the relationship has begun or is a possibility, many of their other symptoms and dispositions can halt or reverse the progress made in the relationship. Fear of rejection and humiliation is strongest when facing someone you have ideas of forming an intimate bond with. The mere idea, even, can be stressful enough. Stacked with the expectations of failure, low self-esteem, and the reluctance to even meet others, intimate relationships are nearly impossible.

Destroying a relationship is also a possibility. Moving forward in any level of intimacy is a personal risk and takes overcoming many inhibitions in it. By limiting the interactions that are capable of creating these moments, the person is then preventing themselves from ever having or keeping a serious relationship.

8. Living through Fantasy

One of the biggest enablers of Avoidant Personality Disorder is the Internet. There is no better way to physically avoid people, prevent one from dealing with personal humiliation, and to create what is thought to be the person everyone would accept, than to use the Internet. Social networks and dating sites allow for the creation of a profile of one's choosing, wherein one can decide what they want to be true and what they want to hide. Pictures are enhanced and changed with software. Gaming characters add a deeper level of fantasy and falsification to the created persona through which the person can live vicariously. In creating another person, they are dodging and covering their own insecurities and psychological issues by presenting a different self. Though this can be an outlet for socialization for someone with AvPD, it also allows them to pretend they do not have a disorder or illness that prevents them from interacting with people in a realistic fashion. Hiding behind a falsified self is a way to allow denial to take over and the person can become even more isolated in the physical world. On the other side of this is the issue brought up earlier about people's own willingness to be crueler in the virtual realm than they would be in reality. Hiding behind a screen name or character gives you a false sense of bravery and thus can lead to bitter results. Even if an AvPD patient has a synthetic self virtually, that self can be just as crippled by the insults and vulgarities of other people. This can be even doubly crippling as they would see their only outlet as being compromised by the same fears in real life that are now coming forth online. Living through fantasy is not an escape, but a setup for a larger regression when something bad happens between them and another person online.

9. Avoidance of Occupational Interpersonal Situations

Having a means for gaining income is integral to surviving in the modern age. With a job comes the necessary interaction between people. Even work-at-home jobs have a client base for it to be profitable. Avoidant Personality Disorder can make almost any job seem daunting. If a person with AvPD has no choice but to work in a place where others frequent, they may not be able to maintain their employment. At the other end of the spectrum, they may be able to work with others but have difficulty relating to other people, speaking up for themselves in certain situations, and taking personal risks to try to advance. Someone with AvPD will often find themselves staying low on the totem pole in jobs as they are unwilling to face the possibilities of rejection and humiliation that go with career advancement. Work-related gatherings, dealing with customers and any other aspect in which confrontation or any type of human interaction is necessary can be something people with Avoidant Personality Disorder are unable to deal with. As a result, employment can be very difficult for patients with AvPD.

Chapter 5: Seven Common Therapy Methods for AvPD

1. Online Support Groups

The Internet can provide ample resources for people with various types of issues. There is a plethora of support groups for almost any disorder, condition, or problem. Having people that understand what one is going through can be a huge help. Oftentimes, in order for someone to even try to get help, the first step is understanding that there is something wrong. Finding others that suffer from similar or the same conditions can help a person understand their own conditions. There is also a benefit in trying to sort through what one can and cannot deal with on their own by having other people, who think the same way, assisting you. This can work two-fold as people often find ways to deal with their own problems whilst helping someone else with similar issues.

2. Group Therapy

Group therapy can be a difficult step with Avoidance Personality Disorder. First of all, there is the fact that it involves other people. The idea that these people are going through the same problems as the patient can somewhat alleviate the fears, but not completely diminish them. Secondly, though others may experience the same issues, the pessimism that occurs with AvPD may leave the patient feeling as if others will still let them down and the same fears will be applied to this group. If the patient can get past the group setting, and this by no means is the first or even second step in the therapeutic process, then being able to relate to others can have a huge positive impact in getting through their difficulties.

3. Exposure Therapy

Group therapy can be considered a type of exposure therapy, but not a significant example. Exposure therapy is the utilization of the person's fears in small doses that are increased gradually over a period of time. This could be something as simple as meeting a new person or going to a public, but not frequented, location. The type of places the person goes to can increase the amount of people typically at those locations. Thus, it is essential to expose the patient to a group of people that becomes larger as the therapy progresses. Exposure therapy can also progress using only people. Depending on the severity of the disorder, the person together with the therapist may be asked to meet with a friend or acquaintance and then maybe someone they hardly know. Eventually this can lead to meeting a completely new person, or someone of the opposite sex. The exposure is a way for the person to face their fears in tolerable amounts in order to see the futility in being so afraid of the situation.

4. Intervention

In reality, the first step in any help for someone with Avoidance Personality Disorder is an intervention of the way they are currently living their life. If the person is unable to see a problem or find help on their own, friends or family should try to intervene. Sometimes people do not often see what is right in front of them, especially when they live a life of seeing things differently from other people. When friends or family begin to see a strong withdrawal, especially when it turns into self-isolation, they need to start taking steps to help their loved one recognize that there is an issue and that help is needed. Unfortunately, those doing what they think are in the best interest of someone they care about can often make things worse. With a patient that has AvPD, taking care not to insult, reject, or humiliate them is important. This means that a well-meaning friend forcing an AvPD friend to attend a movie or go shopping is actually doing more harm than good. The friend does not realize that by forcing someone she cares about to directly face such a large fear at one time can cause the fear to get even more severe. If, instead, the friend slowly introduces a new friend to the AvPD sufferer, and the patient is being introduced in smaller increments, they have a chance to get used to the process of meeting a new person under their current restraints. For the most part, though, intervention should basically focus on helping the person realize that living with AvPD can be tolerable and helping them get professional assistance in overcoming their problems.

5. Cognitive Skills Therapy

Therapists can assist a person in learning the skills they need to interact with other people and in group settings. A person with AvPD often gets so encompassed by their fears, lack of confidence and self-image, and negative outlook that they will actually regress in social skills. Learning how to deal with certain situations, how to approach a new person, how to deal with rejection and humiliation, and over all reacquire the lost social skills is a very useful form of therapy. There is still the drawback of the patient believing they are being made fun of or thinking they are less than other people because of their inability to communicate and function with others. The therapist will have to be make sure the patient understands what they are being helped to overcome and how it is a change made not by inability or stupidity, but a change made out of fear. Cognitive therapy is not teaching someone who is of less intelligence or capability how to be social, but instead re-teaching someone how to overcome fears in certain situations in order to get through with the least amount of negative outcome.

6. Psychological Therapy

One of the best sources for assistance is a professional psychologist or psychiatrist. This allows the person dealing with AvPD to have several advantages. The first is that they are only meeting with a single person whose sole job is to listen and help them. This can help diminish some of the fears of dealing with a new person or being judged. It can take a longer period of time for the patient to open up to the doctor, but it can also happen rather fast once the patient feels secure in their standing with the professional. A one-on-one therapeutic session gives the doctor a chance to understand the severity of the patient's current state of mind and can allow the patient time to get acclimated to talking about their fears under confidentiality. A professional can help find the initial cause of the irrational feelings, help the patient see where they are struggling in their life and give the patient perspective about how one can live with a condition like AvPD. Professional therapists are also trained to restrain from opinions, judgment, and rejection. This removes a layer of possible negative outcomes from this form of treatment.

7. Drug Therapy

Drug therapy is debatable on two fronts. First, the medical pharmacology use is often misused and can lead to belief in a quick cure-all, an oversight on the underlying issues, or abuse by the patient. Second, the use of recreational drugs has now entered the market and is still not legal nor accepted everywhere. Medical prescriptions can be provided to deal with an AvPD patient's underlying anxiety or depression issues. Once these issues have been regulated, especially in the case of a chemical imbalance, learning how to overcome the psychological aspects can be approached. With prescriptions, though, there is a high possibility of abuse. Making sure medical drug regulation is abided by is integral to the process. The use of marijuana, or even other alternative healing methods, can cause many problems. Patients need to make sure they function under the laws of their area before proceeding with any alternative therapies. They also need to consider how it can be worse for them. One important fact is the ability of marijuana to cause paranoia in people, especially those with underlying anxiety disorders. Another factor is the stigma that some people place on alternative medicine and how there is a possibility for further humiliation or problems with other people. This being said, marijuana is making huge progress in the medical field for assisting with the tolerance of pain, depression, anxiety, and even terminal issues. The only way to determine which treatment would benefit one best is to see a doctor and discuss the physical and mental disorders at hand and determining, together, what would be the most beneficial treatment.

Chapter 6: How to Choose the Right Therapy Approach

Before choosing a therapy that would work, AvPD sufferers need to decide how they feel most comfortable in approaching the problems they are facing. The higher the severity of fears about public and group interaction, the more likely they are in need of seeking one-on-one assistance. If the patient is confident in their decision to get help and feel comfortable moving at a different pace, then group therapy or exposure therapy is a viable choice, but it can still be dangerous to jump right into either of those. Another factor is the person's support group of friends and family. This may be a much more viable choice depending on whether they have friends and family to help. A big factor in therapies, unfortunately, is affordability.

Someone that has put themselves into self-isolation and are unable to cope with new people or groups, need to have a slower therapy that starts with the singular focus on them. Easing a patient into social situations is necessary to keep them from backsliding or becoming even more isolated. This is why, even though a patient may think they can jump into group therapy or exposure therapy, they usually need to begin with a one-on-one session with a professional. Having a professional take the time to understand the basis of the disorder, the main fears of the patient, and how the patient would respond to different situations, is important for the healing process. A patient that was traumatized amongst a group of peers would not succeed in being rushed into group therapy. Regardless of the fact that the other participants are there for the same reason, the inability to rationalize reactions and the prominence of pessimism from the others could create a disaster. One of the best ways for someone to overcome initial fears of dealing with those that have AvPD as well is to get online and seek out forums or groups in which AvPD patients talk openly about their fears and issues. This gives the patient a chance to test the waters and gain reaction through the virtual world prior to exposing themselves physically to such groups, in reality. Once a patient feels comfortable with solo sessions with professionals and with talking to others online, then they are more prepared to begin a group-oriented therapy or an exposure therapy that slowly introduces them to multiple people.

Avoidant Personality Disorder would be something quite apparent to close friends and family members. As they will be the first to notice, it is important that they act on behalf of their loved one. Talking to the person directly may or may not be effective. An AvPD patient will be very defensive and most likely, be easily offended by any hint that there is something wrong with them. They do know and they do try to live in a state of denial. AvPD, though, is something that is formed out of fears, so the person will know that they are purposely avoiding common human interaction based on fears that most people do not have. This gives credence to the idea that they have a unique situation to their immediate peer group. With this knowledge, the confrontation would need to be well thought out. The last thing a loved one wants to do is to hurt the patient more. The focus should be on being worried about the patient, especially of them being alone all the time. There should be points made about the hindrances the person faces in simple daily activities, like grocery shopping or even working, that also concern the family member or friend. The one factor that can be detrimental to friend and family intervention is the reason behind the person's disorder. A history of familial neglect or abuse would make family intervention a very bad decision. In fact, it could make the situation much worse for the patient.

Consider the history of the person's illness before focusing on how to help them get better.

If the family (or even the patient themselves) knows that the condition is something the patient's parents have as well, this is a good time to bring up medical assistance. Medication can be vital in controlling underlying anxiety and depressive disorders. Especially if the person is suicidal or has disturbing thoughts of hurting themselves or others, medical assistance will be vital to helping them. Even if the condition is not genetic, a predominance of depression or anxiety can be treated with medication and give the person a boost to help them go about overcoming their illness. Not everyone needs medication, and if the patient is not showing serious signs of anxiety or depression, then medication is unnecessary. On the other hand, a patient showing extreme levels of depression or anxiety may need to stay in a facility until a medication regimen is found and proven effective in order to prevent harm to the person or others around them.

One of the biggest problems today is cost of care. If one is in need of legitimate psychological therapy or of medical therapy, insurance or assistance may be necessary in getting the care. Assistance from friends, family, and online support groups are really the only inexpensive ways to go about getting help. From there a therapist would have to be found based on their specialty and insurance coverage or base price. Doctors for medical treatment can be found in county facilities or through welfare if the person does not have insurance. Regardless, someone with AvPD should always search for a source of help. Price can be variable and there are places where financial assistance is available. Asking others to help can be very difficult for someone with Avoidant Personality Disorder, and so they will not usually come forward with such a request. Again, it may be necessary for the people around them to help in a comforting and concerned manner.

Chapter 7: How to Overcome AvpD: 7 Steps

1. Intervention

Intervention is the first step in dealing with Avoidance Personality Disorder. By definition, the condition is one in which the person is avoiding the things they have difficulty dealing with. With this in mind, the AvPD patient is much less likely to seek out help on their own. Living in a constant state of denial, the person dealing with this will not want to acknowledge how far they have descended into their false sense of reality. This leaves other people around them to initiate the changes to be made, in most circumstances. The problem there then lies with the approach. The one thing that can make an intervention ineffective would be making the person feel even worse about themselves, doubting their ability to overcome the disorder, or feeling humiliation at people noticing their difficulties. Caution is to be used when trying to intervene with AvPD patients. They need to feel comfortable with the person intervening. They also need to feel that the intervention is coming from people caring about them and worrying about them. Focusing on the person suffering, concerned individuals need to give special care to the patient's mental state at all times. This is not a situation for tough love or cruelty. Showing compassion, giving the person confidence in their ability to fight back and resume control of their life, and making sure all the support they need is provided, will go a long way in helping them begin the process of overcoming Avoidant Personality Disorder.

2. Admission

Once or if there is an intervention, the patient must now come to the conclusion that they do in fact have a problem. If an intervention is not made, then this is the first step in fighting back. Admission goes against their ingrained denials on the life they live. Often they will bring up the fact that it is easier to avoid situations than risk being hurt by them. Though this does make some sense, it is not safe or healthy to keep avoiding people your entire life. Being around other people is integral to living a healthy life. The patient needs to see that living in false realities, staying away from contact, and self-isolation, is not only unhealthy, but against their biological nature as a social creature. Depression is worse when the person remains in an isolated state. Coming to terms with there being a problem, and that denial no longer works, is the next step in the healing process.

3. Understanding

Understanding their condition and how much of what they feel and experience is part it, is the next crucial step. If one does not understand the full extent of how something is affecting their life, they may not see the need to make a change. Learning about depression, anxiety, and their phobias will help them see how many of these components equate to the misery they maintain. Education about any problem can be done online. There are ample resources for information, studies, therapies, and discussions on almost any topic. Researching Avoidant Personality Disorder should be an important part of overcoming the illness. The patient must learn how each area of their lives has been changed and how their very outlook on the world around them is not typical. They must learn what causes the issues of AvPD and how these causes lead to the symptoms that have created their current lifestyle. Understanding the disorder also gives patients a chance to see that the problem is not them as a person, the problem is how their brain processes and either accepts or denies certain circumstances and information. They need to learn about constructive criticism, common banter between friends, dealing with rejection and criticism, and, most importantly, how to accept themselves.

4. Symptom Evaluation

Now that the patient has come to terms that there is a problem and they have learned about Avoidant Personality Disorder, they need to seek a professional for an official diagnosis and an evaluation of their symptoms. Truthfully, a diagnosis should not be made by anyone who is not a professional. Despite this, intervention, acceptance, and understanding can be found just by knowing that there is a problem with how they accept and deal with reality. They do not need to necessarily be researching Avoidant Personality Disorder as much as they should be researching their symptoms and how they can be dealt with. Once they seek the advice of a professional, their symptoms can be fully recognized. Putting together the different symptoms, the professional can then come to a diagnosis of a behavioral or personality disorder.

AvPD may be more specific than the professional diagnosis, but the fact that an issue is not only found and understood but declared by someone who has studied such things can help set the patient's mind at ease. Also, symptoms that would stand out to a professional may not be obvious to patients. A patient may not realize their obsession with false online worlds as being a symptom. They may also not understand that physical problems under certain circumstances, like headaches and nausea in public, are attributes of the disorder. With a professional, symptoms can be discovered, put together, and the full picture can be seen and understood.

5. Therapy

Now that there is a diagnosis, treatment is in order. The doctor initially visited will probably be the one to suggest medication and therapy for the patient. Once again, if the patient feels uncomfortable with the prescribed medication, they should seek another opinion or try to discuss it with their doctor. In many cases, medication will be administered strictly to help deal with the overt anxiety or depression so that the patient can move on to dealing with the psychological problems. Once a therapist is seen, they will have a session with the patient to decide how to proceed from that point. They may feel that the patient needs a series of one-on-one sessions and then move on to exposure or group therapy. They may decide to put the patient, if they feel it is safe to do so, straight into group therapy. The good thing about dealing with any medical professional or therapist is that they are there to listen to the patient and help them overcome these issues in the most successful path. Sessions may come at a weekly or bi-monthly basis or be more or less often. The therapist will be able to evaluate the patient's capabilities to tolerate certain circumstances and together they can lay out a plan to successfully help the patient find a way to live a better life with AvPD.

6. Support

A particularly important aspect to the healing of any patient dealing with psychological disorders is support. People who deal with issues of their mental state need to have a strong support system. Doctors and therapists make up a portion of this system. If a doctor or therapist does not seem to be a good listener or is not being supportive, it is highly encouraged that the patient seeks another professional to help them. It is completely unnecessary and against patient rights for someone to tolerate a doctor that is not fully committed to the patient's well-being. The professionals are only a small part of the support group, though. Family and friends are very important to the patient. Having anyone criticize or humiliate the patient will be severely harmful to the patient's mental state. They need positive reinforcement, confidence, and dependability. Avoidance Personality Disorder is seeded in the idea that people will hurt them and let them down. Having anyone close to them do exactly this will only create a severe backslide that can leave the patient in a worse condition than they originally started with. Support is crucial and will be necessary later when the person is ready to try to reintroduce themselves to public and social situations. Having someone they can depend on with whom they are secure will not hurt them will allow them more freedom to face their fears.

7. Adherence

The patient has now understood that there is a problem, faced the reality of the disorder and what it has done to their lives, sought professional help, and gained a support system. The rest is up to the patient. Sticking with the therapies and doing their best not to fall back into bad habits of self-depreciating and self-isolating is extremely important. A person suffering from Avoidant Personality Disorder has a lot to cope with and the healing process takes time. Impatience will not lead to success. Maintaining contact with good and dependable support people and keeping therapeutic schedules is part of the adherence. The patient should be careful not to over-stimulate themselves either. Feeling the freedom of overcoming the fears that had led to their previous lifestyle can sometimes make the person think they can deal with situations that might back fire. An example of this would be going to a crowded event or facing someone that had been a source of humiliation or rejection. By pushing themselves they are leaving the possibility of being hurt again and falling back on old habits. If there is a regression, it is vital for the person to turn to their support group, professionals and personal circle of familiar people, to help them overcome the setback. Once again, this is why caution needs to be taken in facing challenges. Baby steps may seem to take too long, but it has the smallest failure rate. Being that people with AvPD are used to avoiding personal risks, it is usually natural for them to accept a slower and easier pace of healing and they are less likely to try to face such a big challenge. Those situations usually arise from pressure from others. Feeling the need to appease certain people could cause the patient to wrongfully follow the advice and thus can lead to the setback. Overall, sticking to the plan set down by the doctor and/or therapist is the best bet.

Chapter 8: How to Find Your Escape

Avoidant Personality Disorder can have many symptoms and the people that have with the disorder can deal with it in many different ways. Regardless of the symptoms and the tolerance of the sources of the problem, someone with AvPD needs to have a way to escape the fears and stresses they are constantly dealing with. The source of AvPD lies in dealing with other people and socialization. In order to have a cool down time, people with AvPD need to have a way to relax and have time in which the disorder has no bearing. Though being isolated, alone, or living through fantasy is a reaction to AvPD, it does not mean that those moments should not be taken or allowed. Reading, writing, nature walks, and hobbies can help lower stress and anxiety. Writing can be very helpful as the person can release a lot of their fears, worries, thoughts, and problems into an outlet that has no way to humiliate or reject them. Finding a hobby that they enjoy can also help with their self-depreciation issues. People who do something they like, regardless of how good they are at it, can often find the hobby soothing and find reassurance in their own capabilities. This can be even more beneficial if it is a hobby they can profit from without having to expose themselves to other people. Crafting, art work, writing, and other home-based projects can become a source of income as well as a way to decompress from outside stress and depression. Many sufferers of depression find outlets in some form of artistic talent because of the way they can use their pain to create something that they or even others can appreciate.

Another useful practice for someone with AvPD is meditation. Learning how to calm your inner sorrows and fears by calming your mind can be very beneficial. Meditation utilizes soothing music, atmospheres, and relaxation techniques to help people slow down the outside world and find a sense of inner peace. For someone that spends a lot of time alone fretting about the outside world, practicing a way to quiet these inner qualms can help them go great lengths at finding a source of happiness. Meditation is something that can easily be done anywhere, does not need to have anyone present, and does not really need anything other than the person and a setting that they can find quiet time in. There are several ways to meditate and it can be as easy as sitting still somewhere to creating a specific environment. Some people utilize music, fountains, certain noises, incense and/or candles, and other relaxing additives to make their meditation session as peaceful as possible The most difficult part is learning to clear your mind and to find a form of solitude. Once someone has figured out the best approach to meditation for them, the process becomes fairly simple and can even be used to stop panic attacks, calm down from an upsetting situation, or even just find peace before trying to nap or face a situation they are concerned about.

Avoidant Personality Disorder patients should find a past time or hobby that makes them happy relaxed and gives them a sense of peace. In this way they can escape the pains and frustrations of AvPD and find a source of positivity in their life.

Conclusion

Living a life in fear of other people is something no one should have to endure. Though it is not the people themselves that are being feared, the socialization with people can cause serious damage to someone with Avoidant Personality Disorder. Phobias linked to dealing with criticism and rejections are prominent with AvPD. The current functionality of society and how people approach others allow ample opportunities for someone to be hurt by another person's lack of feelings about what they are saying. AvPD patients go through life avoiding contact with other people. They stay away from groups and public places, personal risk is something they are not willing to make, and their inhibitions and reluctance at having meaningful relationships stem from these fears of rejection and mental pain. Overall, it is a severely debilitating disorder.

Living the life of a loner or hermit can seem appealing, but it is not so easy when the very idea of dealing with face to face contact with other people causes stress. Avoidant Personality Disorder can create a downward spiral in which the person will withdraw, turn negative focus inward, and eventually try to live life through virtual personas or in an agoraphobic lockdown. The use of fantasy characterizations can create false actualization in people with AvPD. What this means is that the person living through a fake and created personality will come to live in a known state of denial about themselves. They will see the positive aspects of their creations as a determining factor of their own personal failings. They are not delusional in thinking they are the character; they believe they can only be successful in socialization by being the character. This leads to a false sense of self in which they are highlighting the negative aspects of their own personality and amplifying them. Again a cycle is created and their self-esteem continues to plummet as they rely on a fake profile to represent who they think they should be. This backfires as people in general gain a false sense of bravado in the virtual worlds. People tend to be crueler, harsher, and more vulgar when they are hiding behind a fake name, character, or profile. This is how many people cope with social anxiety and conditions like AvPD, in order to try to socialize without actually coming in contact with people in their everyday life.

The more someone with AvPD withdraws, the harder it is to extract them from the dark cave of their own fears and reluctance at interaction. This can be very devastating if the person with AvPD has depression issues, as suicidal tendencies and thoughts can be a part of their condition. Facing their fears can make the situation much worse and then causes a much bigger withdrawal, if at all possible. Living a life devoid of other human contact causes strain on personal life and working environments, more so if there is not a working or personal environment for them to even be evolved in. The cage that an AvPD patient creates for themselves is one of a warped reality. They see themselves as unable to interact, not worth being a part of society, and that they are a subpar person. Trying to overcome these ingrained feelings and beliefs is the crux of overcoming Avoidant Personality Disorder.

There are many ways that Avoidant Personality Disorder can be overcome, but this does not come without its own risks. Medication can help if there is an underlying depression or anxiety issue with the patient. This is especially useful in cases where there is genetic disposition to have these mental illnesses. Therapy is the prime way to deal with AvPD and there is a multitude of ways to approach different therapeutic styles to begin the healing process. Having friend and family to support and help a person through

AvPD is another crucial aspect to overcoming the limitations set down by the disorder.

In conclusion, Avoidant Personality Disorder is a mental illness that completely separates a person from society. Someone with this condition will suffer from low self-esteem, depression, anxiety, irrational fears, and an inability to deal with the prospect of facing a negative interaction with other people. As the condition progresses, they may find themselves unable to cope at work or school, unable to face crowds in public, and even unable to socialize with friends and family. This will eventually lead to more serious issues like severe depression, agoraphobia, and even suicidal tendencies. In some cases there are even diagnoses of schizophrenia, multiple personality disorder, and self-mutilation. With the right support network, therapists, doctors, and/or medication, someone suffering from Avoidant Personality Disorder may be able to overcome the disorder and maintain a functioning lifestyle. Maintaining their upswing in trying to change for the better is crucial for them to continue to improve. Regardless of the extent of the disorder, it is something that can be overcome and once they have done so, patients with AvPD can finally be able to live a life of normalcy.

Final Word/About the Author

I was born and raised in Norwalk, Connecticut. Growing up, I could often be found spending afternoons reading in the local public library about management techniques and leadership styles, along with overall outlooks towards life. It was from spending those afternoons reading about how others have led productive lives that I was inspired to start studying patterns of human behavior and self-improvement. Usually I write works around sports to learn more about influential athletes in the hopes that from my writing, you the reader can walk away inspired to put in an equal if not greater amount of hard work and perseverance to pursue your goals. However, I began writing about psychology topics such as Avoidant Personality Disorder so that I could help others better understand why they act and think the way they do and how to build on their strengths while also identifying their weaknesses. If you enjoyed

Avoidant Personality Disorder: The Ultimate Guide to Symptoms, Treatment, and Prevention, please leave a review! Also, you can read more of my general works on *ISTJs*, ISFJs, ISFPs, INTJs, *INFPs, ENFJs, ENFPs, ESFJs, ESTJs, ESFPs, How to be Witty, How to be Likeable, How to be Creative, Bargain Shopping, Productivity Hacks, Morning Meditation, Becoming a Father,* and *33 Life Lessons: Success Principles, Career Advice & Habits of Successful People* in the Kindle Store.

Like what you read?

If you love books on life, psychology, or productivity, check out my website at claytongeoffreys.com to join my exclusive list where I let you know about my latest books. Aside from being the first to hear about my latest releases, you can also download a free copy of *33 Life Lessons: Success Principles, Career Advice & Habits of Successful People.* See you there!

Endnotes

[1] Ekern, MS, LPC, Jacquelyn. "Avoidant Personality Disorder Causes, Statistics, Signs, Symptoms & Side Effects." *Addiction Hope RSS*. 16 Apr. 2013. Web. 4 Mar. 2015. http://www.addictionhope.com/mood-disorder/avoidant-personality.

[2] "Avoidant Personality Disorder Causes, Statistics, Signs, Symptoms & Side Effects." *Addiction Hope RSS*. Phillip W. Long, M.D. Web. 4 Mar. 2015. http://www.addictionhope.com/mood-disorder/avoidant-personality.

Printed in Great Britain
by Amazon